TYNE & WEAR
A COLOURING BOOK

AMBERLEY

First published 2016

Amberley Publishing
The Hill, Stroud
Gloucestershire, GL5 4EP

www.amberley-books.com

Line drawings reproduced from original photography by Caroline Barnsley, Sandra Brack, John & Joyce Carlson, Keith Cockerill, Steve Ellwood, Pat Hope, Margaret Hall, Ken Hutchinson, Michael Johnson, Anthea Lang, Nick Neave, A. W. Purdue, Darren W. Ritson.

British Library Cataloguing in Publication Data.
A catalogue record for this book is available from the British Library.

ISBN 978 1 4456 6133 9 (PRINT)

Typesetting by Amberley Publishing.
Printed in Great Britain.

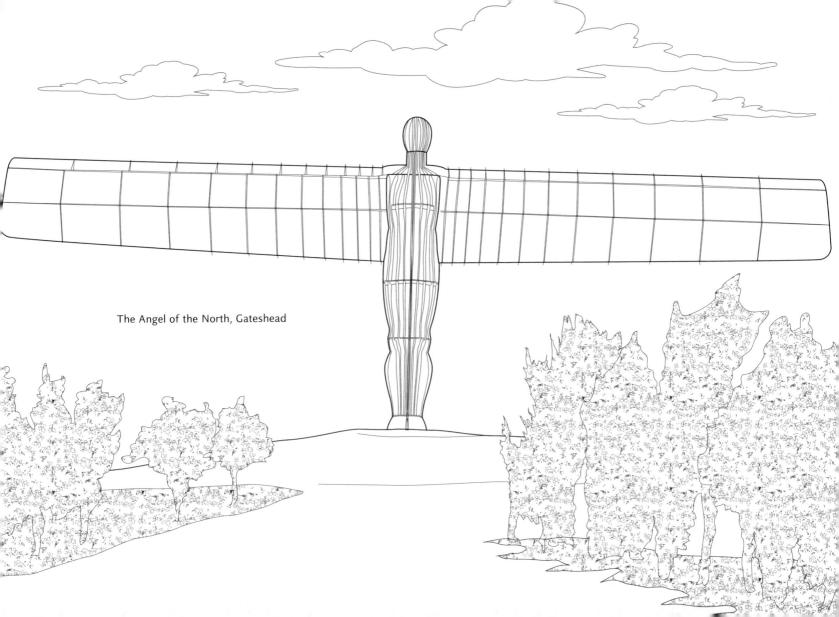

The Angel of the North, Gateshead

Grainger Street, Newcastle, 1904

The *Northumbrian* Ferry

Tynemouth Banks, 1900

The Wear Bridge, Sunderland

Church of St Cuthbert, Haydon Bridge

IN PROUD
AND LOVING
MEMORY OF
THE MEN OF
THE PARISH
OF HAYDON
WHO GAVE
THEIR LIVES
FOR KING
AND COUNTRY

Marsden Bay, South Shields

North Marine Park, South Shields

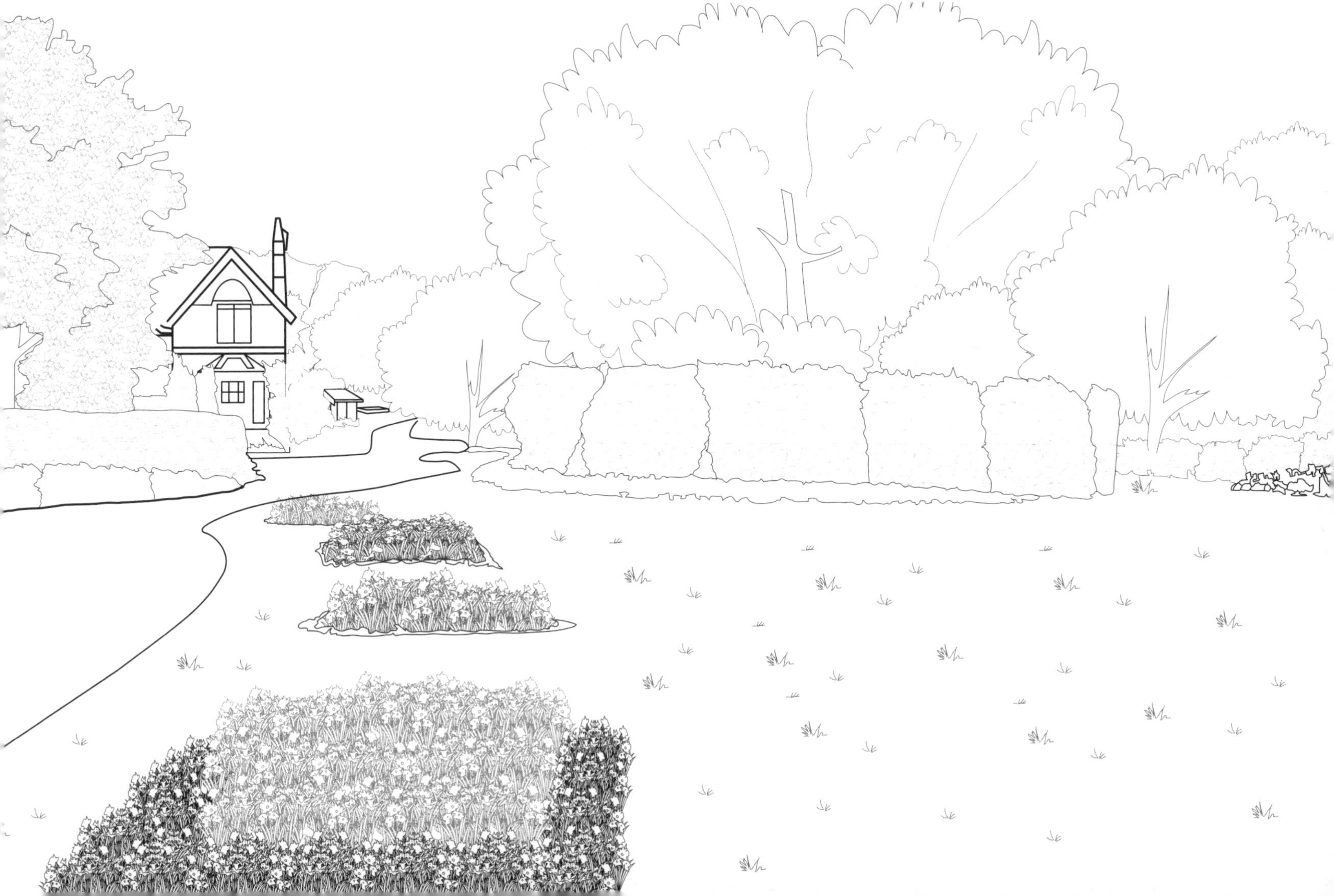

GREETINGS

THE LAKE So. MARINE PARK.

THE PIER.

WOULDHAVE MEMORIAL & TRAM TERMINUS

THE OLD TYPE LIFEBOAT.

SOUTH SHIELDS.

WESTOE VILLAGE.

Lakeshore Railway Road

The Haymarket with St Thomas' Tower and the South African War Memorial, 2011

Harley Mill, Holywell, 2013

The Pleasure Park

The Pier, South Shields

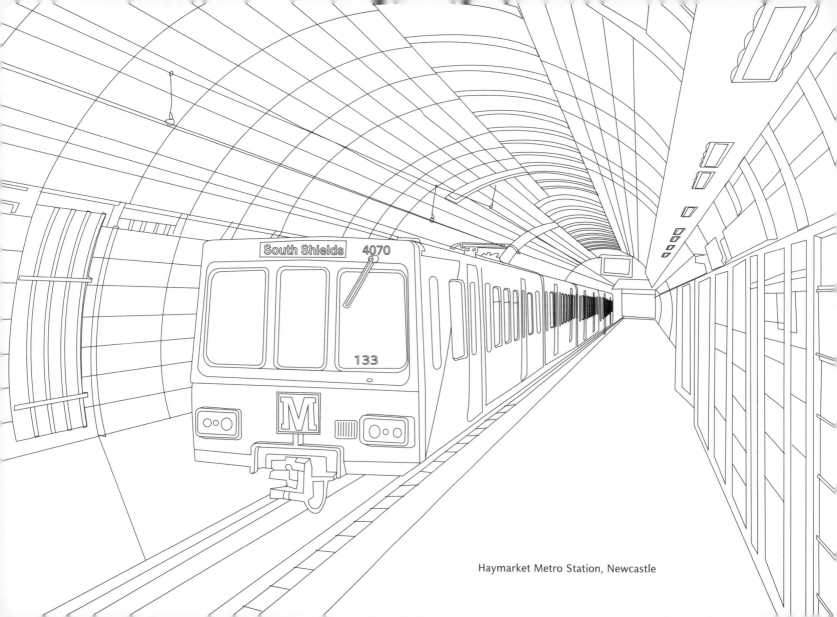

Haymarket Metro Station, Newcastle

The Odeon, Newcastle

Susan Hayward
The LUSTY MEN
PLUS
KON-TIKI

TODAY

GENERAL STATION
VIA NORTH ROAD
31

LBB 50

The Golden Lion, South Shields

Tyne Bridge Under Construction, 1928

Chipchase Castle

St Anthony's Church

BANK

The Cathedrals Express

The Swing Bridge

The Clock Vaults, North Shields

Saltwell Towers, 1876

Whinney House, Low Fell

Lifeboat Memorial, South Shields

The New Town Hall, Gateshead, Opened in 1868

The Close With Some Sheep Being Led to the Quayside, 1898

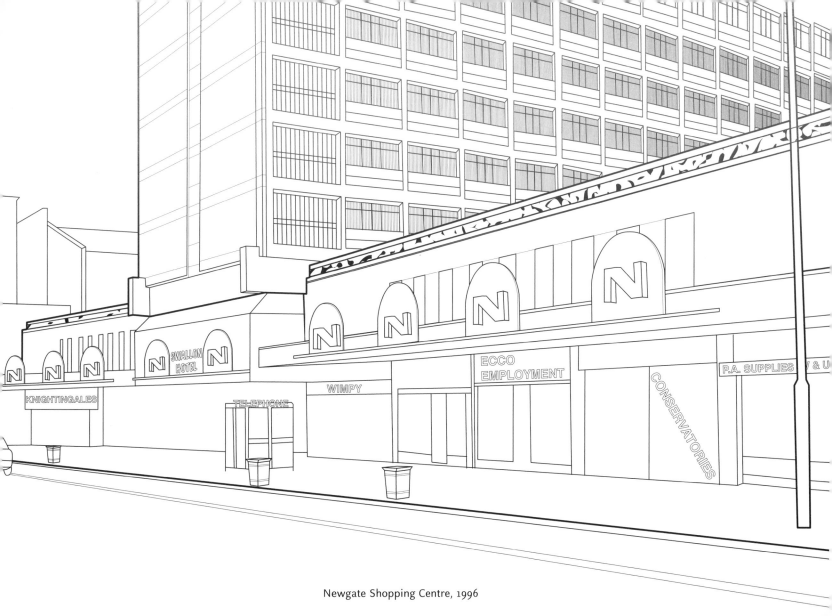

Newgate Shopping Centre, 1996

Gateshead Station, Newcastle

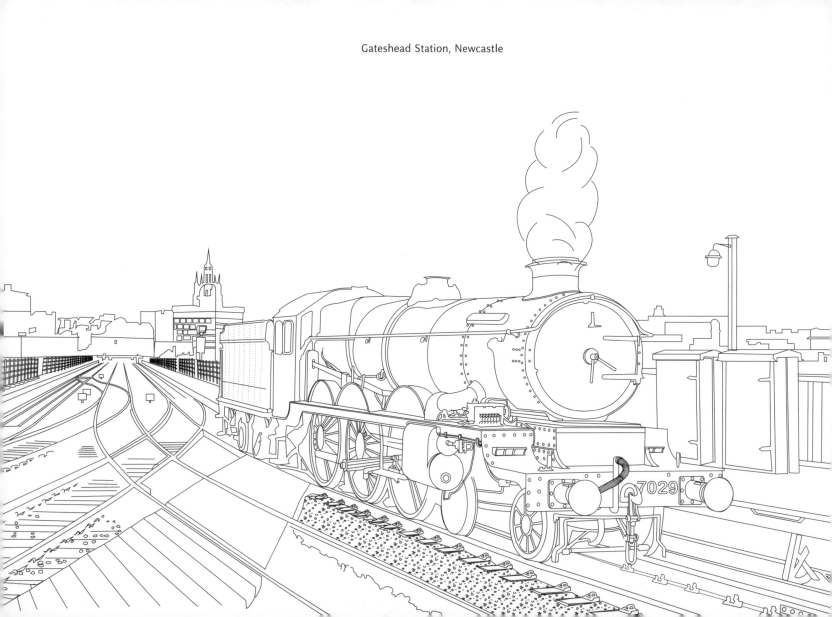

A Local Business Van, South Shields

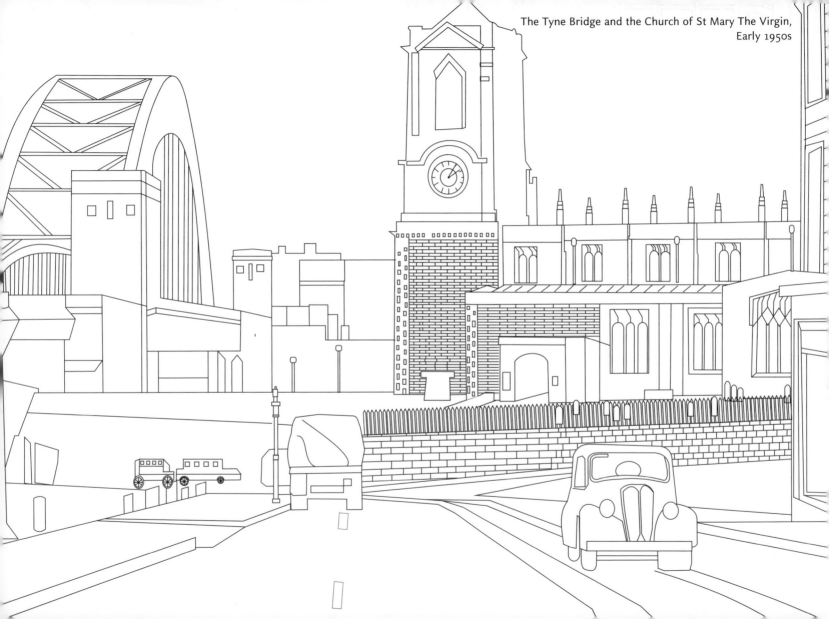

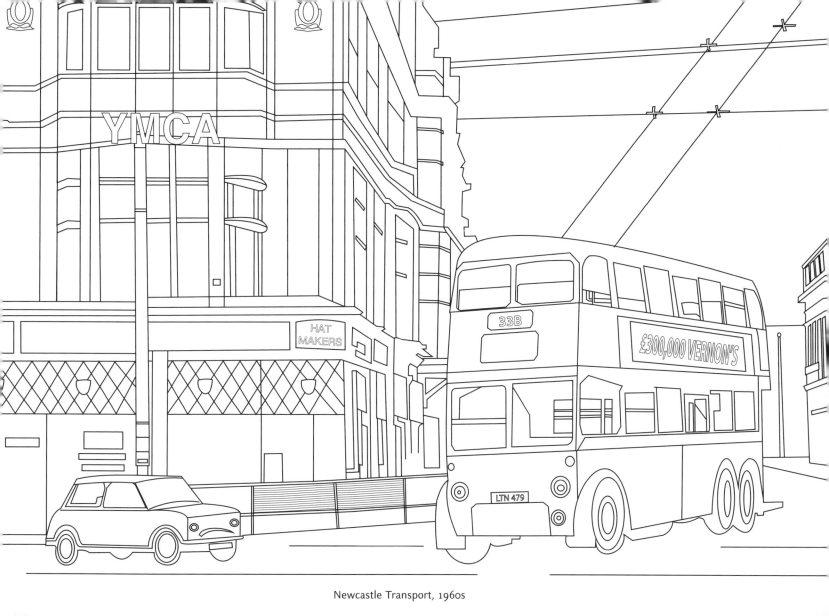

Newcastle Transport, 1960s

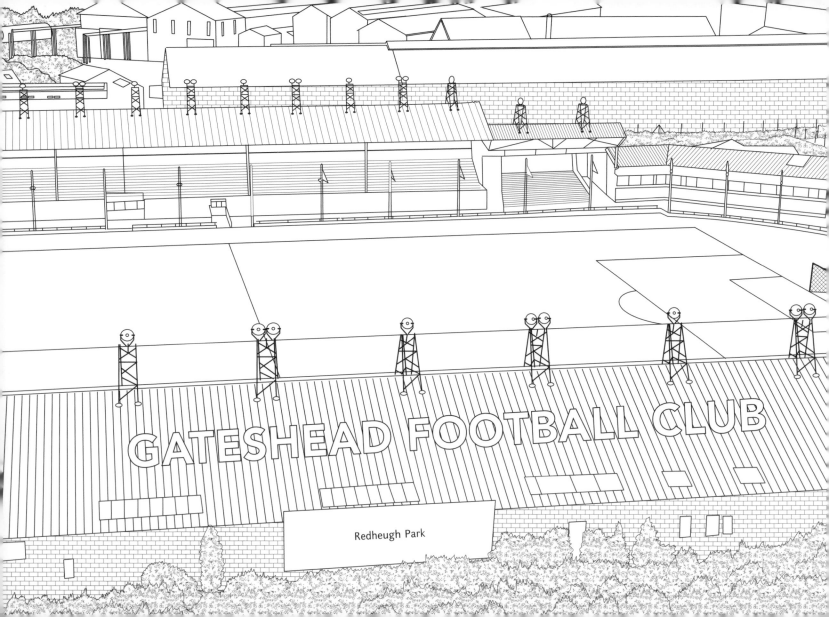

GATESHEAD FOOTBALL CLUB

Redheugh Park

West Park, South Shields

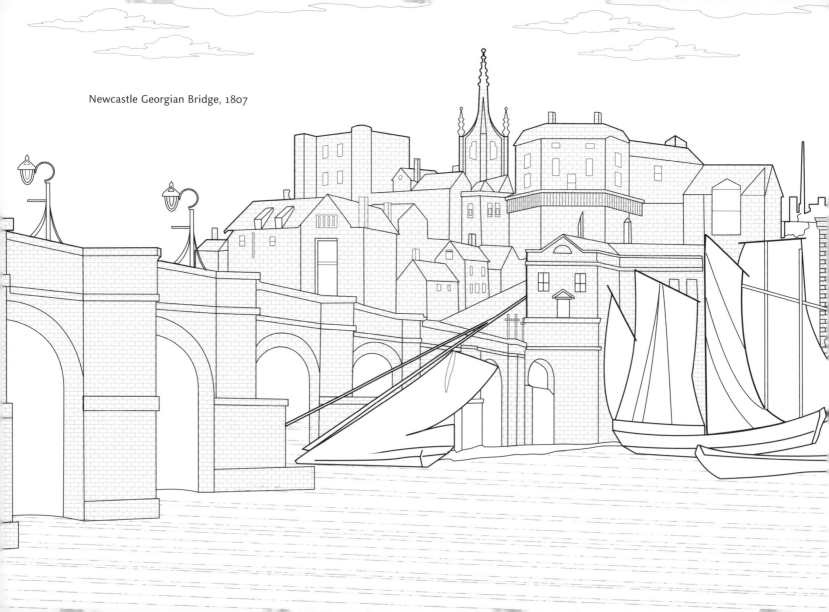

Newcastle Georgian Bridge, 1807

Whitley Park Council Chambers, 1922

Hoggett's Crisps Van, Gateshead, 19

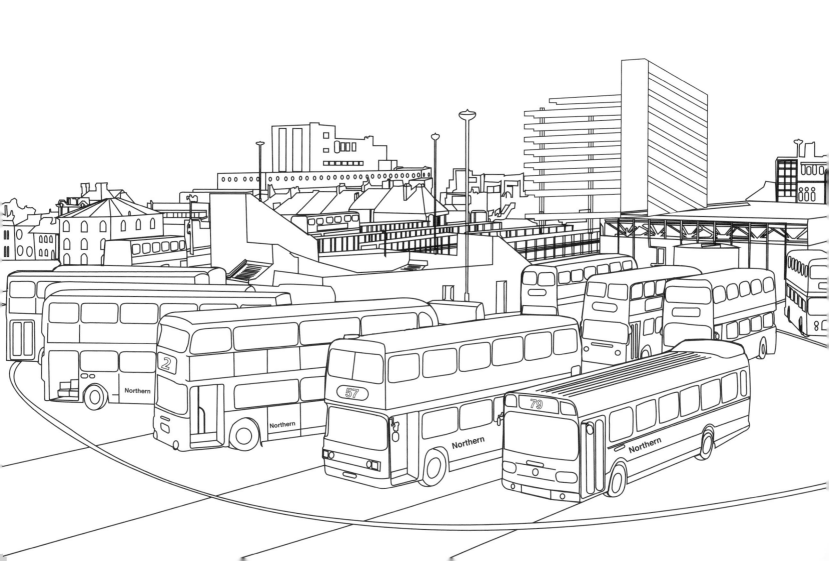

Muir Gardens, Whitley Bay, Before 1909

Fishing Boats and the TS *Wellesley*, South Shields

Royal Jubilee Exhibition, Old Tyne Bridge, 1887

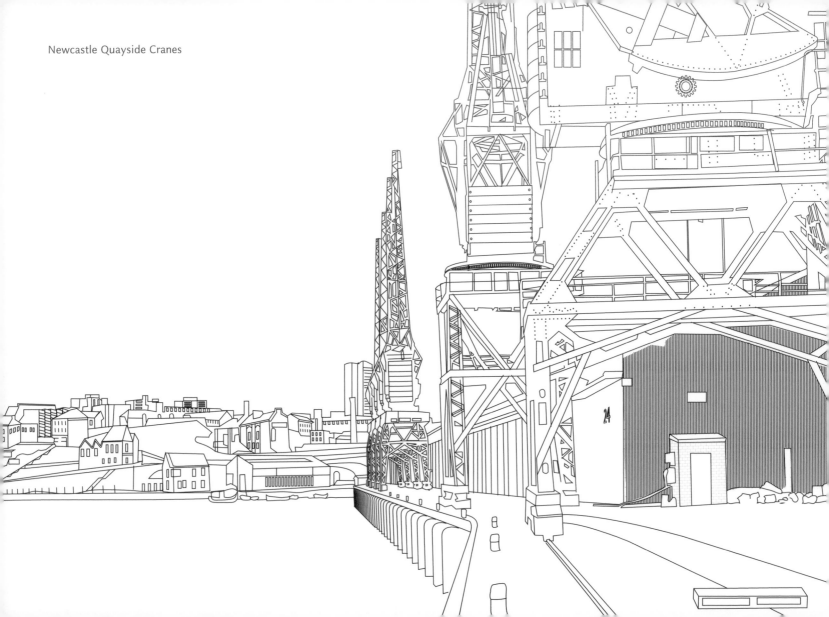

Newcastle Quayside Cranes

Dockwray Square, North Shields

Waterfall, Holywell Dene, 2013

River Scene, Gateshead, 1915

Newcastle in the Early 1800s

Horn & Son Gateshead, 1910

The High Street, 1965

Panama Dip & Empress Ballroom, 1938

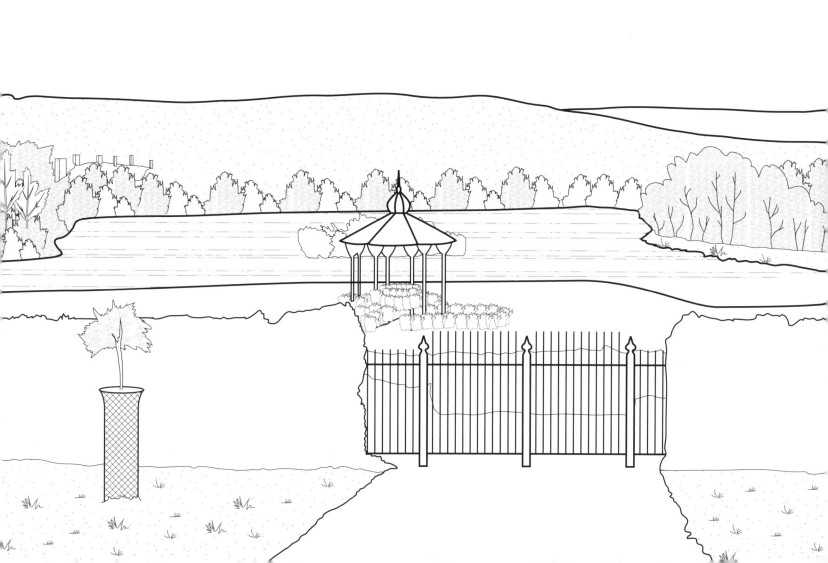

Newcastle Bridges, Looking West

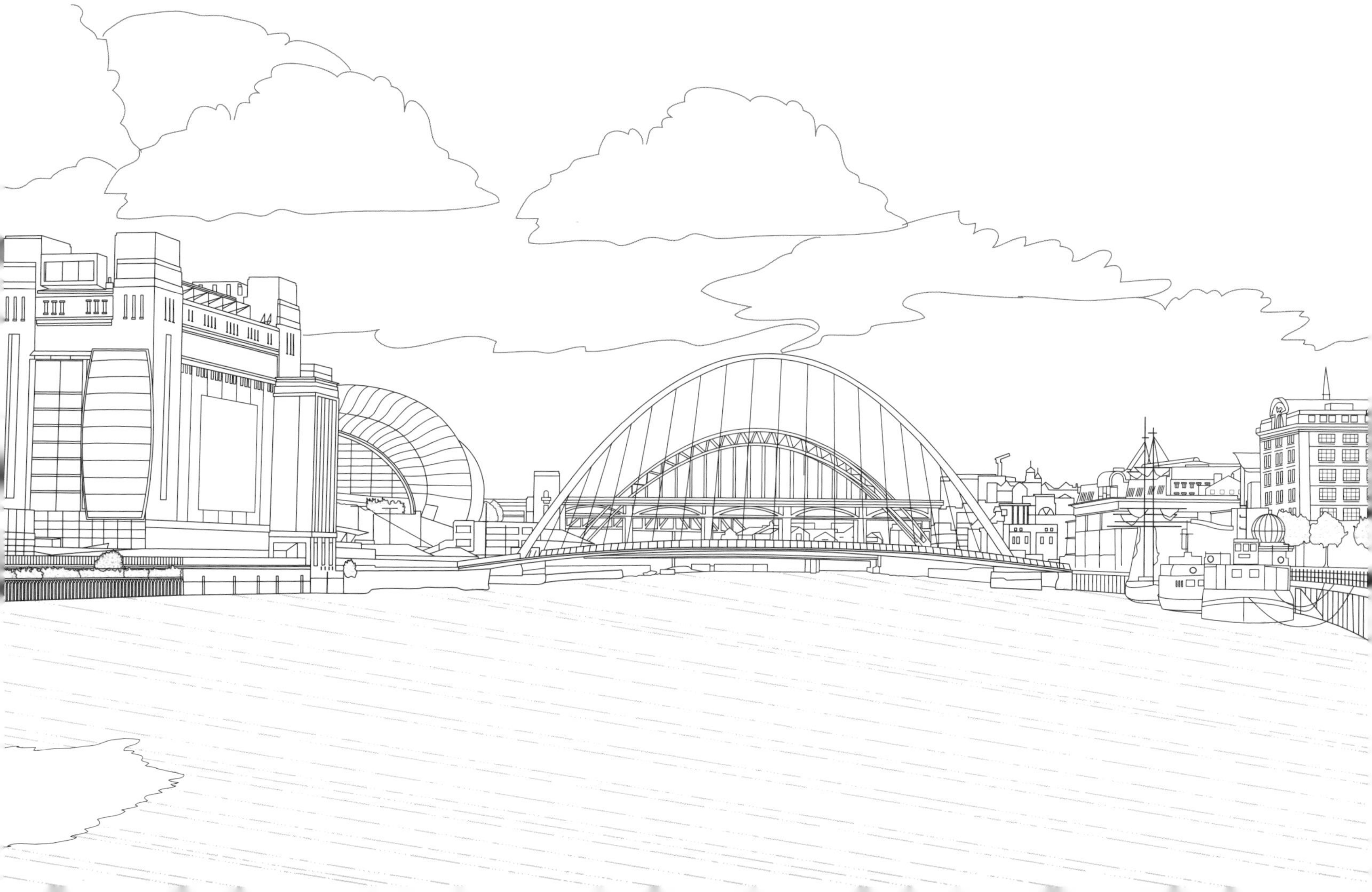

Town Hall, South Shields

The 33 Service to Watson Avenue

Interior of Moon's Garage, Gateshead, 1933

Gateshead East Station, 1952

Guildhall & Fisherman Market From the East, Newcastle

Stockton Terrace, Sunderland, 1905

Central Arcade

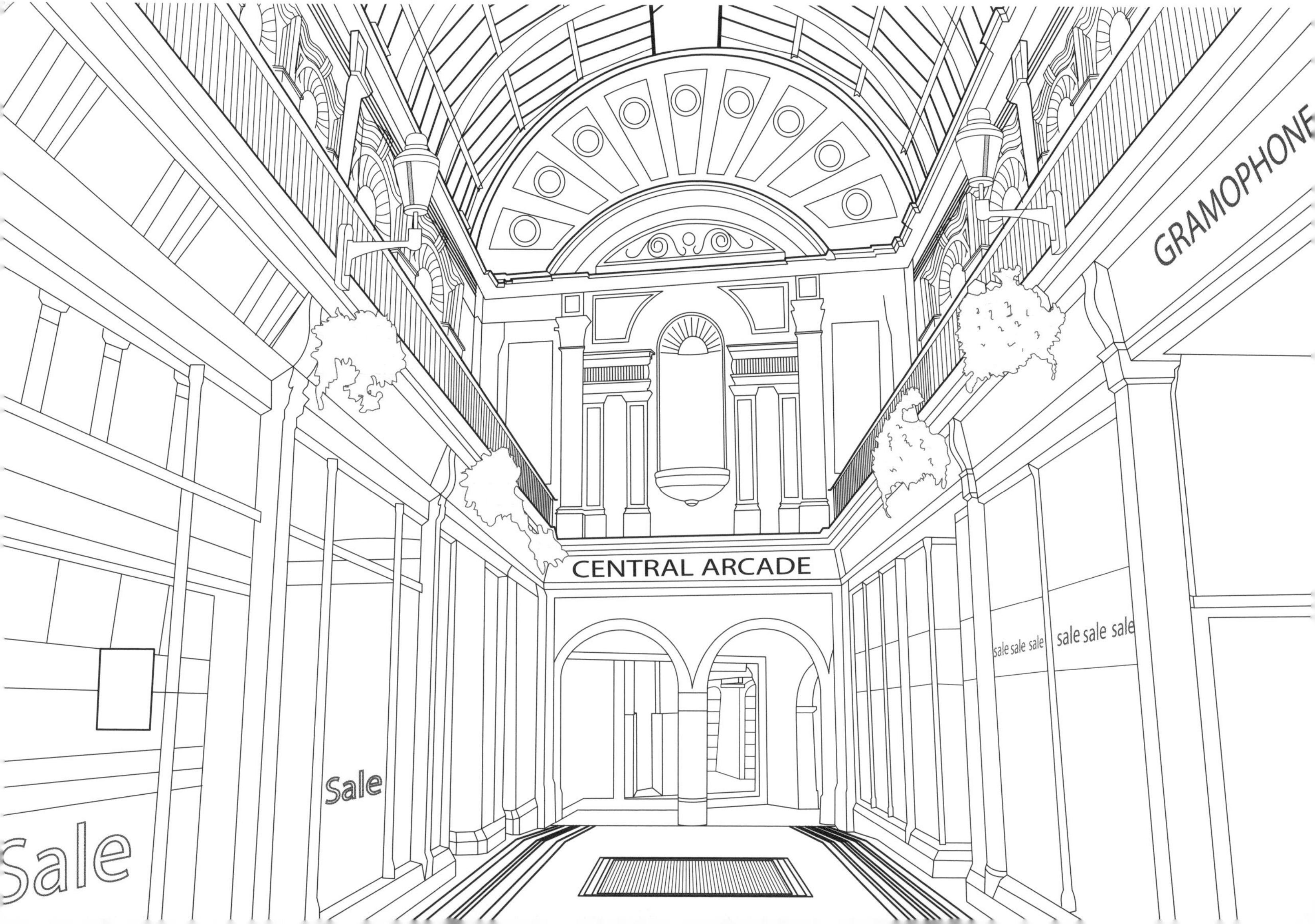

GRAMOPHONE
CENTRAL ARCADE
sale sale sale
sale sale sale
Sale
Sale

Kielder Castle

St Mary's Lighthouse, Whitley Bay

The Sands, Whitley

The Links, Whitley Bay

WHITLEY BAY

PERMARE PERTERRAS

Whitley Road, Whitley Bay